AF126379

BOOK ANALYSIS

Written by Sorène Artaud
Translated by Ciaran Traynor

The Song of the World

BY JEAN GIONO

Bright
≡Summaries.com

JEAN GIONO

FRENCH WRITER

- **Born in Manosque in 1895.**
- **Died in Manosque in 1970.**
- **Notable works:**
  - *The Song of the World* (1934), novel,
  - *Les Âmes fortes* ("Strong Souls", 1950), novel
  - *The Horseman on the Roof* (1951), novel

Jean Giono was a French writer and director who was born in Manosque in 1895. He was called up for military service in 1914, and the scenes he witnessed in the war turned him into a staunch pacifist, to such an extent that he was imprisoned in 1939 for writing pacifist texts. He was then wrongly accused of collaboration with the Nazis in 1945, which led to a certain darkness in his later works. He died in 1970.

His works are characterised by a profound sense of humanism, the veneration of nature and rural life, and a focus on war, and put both man and nature in turn at the heart of their reflections.

He is the author of *Hills of Destiny* (1929), *To the Slaughterhouse* (1931), *The Song of the World* (1934), *Joy of Man's Desiring* (1936) and *The Horseman on the Roof* (1951).

THE SONG OF THE WORLD

A NOVEL IN WHICH YOU CAN "HEAR THE WORLD SING"

- **Genre**: novel
- **Reference edition**: Giono, J. (2000) *The Song of the World*. Trans. Fluchère, H. and Myers, G. California: Counterpoint.
- **1ˢᵗ edition**: 1934
- **Themes**: nature, vengeance, love, family, clans

Published in 1934, *The Song of the World* is the first Jean Giono book which is set in the mountains. It recounts the quest of Antonio, a fisherman by birth, who accompanies his friend Sailor to find the man's lost son. *The Song of The World* is told by an unknown narrator and paints the portrait of valiant, humble men, whose epic journey could rival a Greek myth. However, nature is the real hero of the book, as the author himself wrote in an article in 1932: "For a very long time I have wanted to write a novel in which you could hear the world sing."

SUMMARY

THE TWIN'S DISAPPEARANCE

Having heard nothing from Danis, his "red-haired twin" (p. 5; the other twin is already dead and buried), who left for the Rebeillard country in July, Sailor believes him to be dead, perhaps drowned. However, his son has actually fallen in love with one of the girls of the Maudru clan and has left everything behind to go away with her, thereby attracting a significant number of enemies.

Unable to bear not knowing any longer, Sailor goes to the isle of jays one autumn night to ask Antonio to help him find his son. In the darkness, Antonio goes with him to his house and assures Junie, Sailor's wife, that he will bring back her son. He then goes off into the forest to spend the night.

Antonio goes back to the isle of jays at dawn. Just as Sailor is about to leave, Junie advises him to go to see the almanac-vender when he gets to the Rebeillard country. Before the two meet up, Antonio and Sailor each comb one of the riverbanks for the wayward son. Once night falls, Antonio crosses the river to meet Sailor.

MEETING CLARA

Deep in the forest's murky heart, Antonio and Sailor hear moans coming from somewhere nearby, which turn out to be coming from a woman in childbirth. They later find out that she is blind and her name is Clara. Antonio goes to look for help and comes across the house of the "mother of the road" (p. 50), where he and Sailor take the baby and its mother, who is now very weak. The next day, the mother of the road tells Antonio that some men in the pay of Maudru, the ox-tamer who rules over the town, are also looking for Danis. Antonio and Sailor go to hunt, feeling a little uneasy in Clara's presence. They kill an animal and find themselves face to face with four herdsmen, who leave once they see that some fires have been lit: perhaps the twin has been captured. Antonio holds back Sailor, who wants to set off after them straight away. Before they leave, he asks the mother of the road to look after Clara.

Antonio and Sailor get back on the road before sunrise. They meet a woman on her way to Villevieille with her sick child and accompany her and another man to a little cottage, where they plan to stay the night. However, it turns out that the house is full of sick people, and so the two decide to sleep outside. The next day, they stop in a barn where they meet some sick people who are going to be treated by a man nicknamed "the hunchback".

THE INJURED MAN

The next day, the two friends leave the barn at the same time as the sick people. They help to carry a man who has a stomach injury from a rifle. He turns out to be the nephew of Maudru, Mederic. During the journey, the find out more about the Maudru family: the injured man is the son of Gina, Maudru's sister, who reigns over the Maladrerie estate with an iron fist. He is completely smitten with Maudru's daughter, his cousin who is also called Gina. When he tried to find the man with the red hair who took her away, his rival shot him.

As promised, Sailor and Antonio go to see

Monsieur Toussaint, the almanac-vender, when they get to town. Sailor immediately recognises the "little hunchback with a big head" (p. 136) as Jerome, Junie's brother, who has changed his name and now is something of a doctor. Jerome reveals the twin is staying at his house with Gina, who he has married. He calls the girl, who admits that she regrets having believed and followed Sailor's son, as she now has to live like a fugitive. Toussaint sends a messenger to Junie to tell her that her husband and son are alive and well.

MEDERIC'S DEATH

In the meantime, winter arrives in the Rebeillard country. In order to gather information, Antonio goes to the town inn, where he talks with Maudru's men. He learns that Mederic, the injured man he helped in the barn, is dying from his wound. Gina, his mother, is beside herself with grief and wants to avenge him, sending herdsmen in Maudru's pay to track down the twin.

Antonio has begun to have feelings for Clara and tells Toussaint that he wants to settle down with her. On the way back to his room, he overhears a conversation between young Gina and her husband. He then goes to Sailor's room. His friend cannot sleep, and Antonio tries to comfort him.

The next morning, while the two friends and Sailor's son are washing together, Toussaint comes back from Maudru's house, where he spoke with Mederic just before he died. He says that he can see something of himself in him, and he thinks that the young man truly loved Gina and would have been able to make her happy. In the morning, Antonio goes to the cemetery with one of Maudru's men and promises to dig Mederic's grave. While he is digging, a man who turns out to be Maudru comes up to him and offers him a smoke. The two get along well before the funeral procession arrives.

SAILOR'S DEATH

Spring is on its way and Antonio despairs that he has not heard anything from Clara since he sent a man to fetch her. He is in a very pessimistic mood and suggests to Sailor that they go for a drink. While they are in the town inn, a woman comes in and hides for a few seconds before running off. Antonio, as if in a dream, follows her. He discovers that the messenger has brought Clara back from the forest.

The next day, Toussaint is worried because Sailor did not come home the night before. He goes to look for him with Antonio and Clara, and it does not take them long to find his body. It seems that Sailor was stabbed in the street when he came out of the inn. Toussaint takes him home: he wants to lie the body on the floor so that the twin will see his father and understand.

A SOLID HOUSE

When he discovers his father's body, the twin is determined to avenge his death and drags Antonio with him to the Maudru family's farm. Together, they overpower the men in the entrance and then set the building on fire. As the flames rage around them, the twin tries to kill Maudru, but he is stopped by Antonio, who tells him that it is time to go home with Gina.

The little group go through the forest on a raft. In order to make Gina feel more at ease, Clara tells her how she manages to guess and recognise things without seeing them. At nightfall, the group stops in a field. Once they are alone, Antonio and Clara admit that they love one another. The raft sets off again at dawn and, while the women are sleeping, Sailor's son tells Antonio about his plans to build a solid house. Antonio thinks about his life with Clara.

CHARACTER STUDY

ANTONIO

Antonio can be considered the main character of *The Song of the World*. The novel opens with him ("Antonio walked out to the far end of the island", p. 3) and finishes with his thoughts ("He was thinking that he was going to take Clara in his arms and lie down with her on the earth", p. 312).

A fisherman by birth, he lives alone on the isle of jays in perfect harmony with nature. His knowledge of water has earned him the nickname "man of the river". His other nickname "Golden-Mouth" comes from the fact that he knows how to speak, although, in his opinion, it is because he knows how to "shout louder than the waters" (p. 15). Behind his taciturn, rough nature (which can be seen from his three scars), Antonio appears to be a rather wise man (he is the one who reasons with Sailor when he gets carried away by worry) and is an extremely loyal friend.

He is described on several occasions as a good-looking man in the prime of his life (he is around 40), and he is also capable of tenderness and pure love, as his meeting with Clara proves. During his quest with Sailor, he is torn between his duty as a friend (to support Sailor to the end) and his attraction to Clara, which means that he is not there when Sailor is killed. His sense of honour is strong enough to make him accompany Danis on his quest for vengeance, but not stronger than his humanity, since he spares Maudru after seeing that the man is weak and bitter.

In Giono's universe, Antonio embodies a certain physical (for his beauty and strength) and moral (because he is upright, valiant, loyal and moderate) ideal.

SAILOR

Sailor is a 75-year-old wood-cutter who, as his name implies, used to be a sailor. Unlike Antonio, the "man of the river", he is a man of the forest and is more at ease on land than on water. Having already lost one of his twins and left without news of the other, the worried father asks Antonio for help. He also mentions his wife Junie, a sign that he is thinking of her with his actions: "We must carry him to his mother up there, and then bury him in dry ground in the forest" (p. 7).

During the quest, he finds himself falling apart on several occasions, fearing that something bad will happen to Danis or that his son has done something terrible. There are other clues that Sailor is guided more by his instincts than by logic. During a confrontation with four herdsmen, Antonio worries about his friend's reaction, because he knows that "when things came to fighting, the old wood-cutter was fond of vainglory and flourish" (p. 67).

TOUSSAINT

Toussaint, Junie's brother and Danis' uncle, lives a reclusive life, spending his time treating passing sick people. Described as a "little hunchback with a big head" (p. 136) and as having a "clear and naïve" (p. 135) voice, he is a learned man who relies on books rather than his instincts. As he explains to Antonio, "there are truths you can sense [...] and there are truths which I know" (p. 173).

Although he only makes a few appearances in the book, Toussaint still leaves a melancholy mark on the story, combined with a pessimistic asceticism not unlike that of a religious man condemned to solitude: "Alone. Alone in time, alone on earth. I can die tomorrow without leaving anybody's heart feeling empty" (p. 173). Toussaint talks like a man who has given up on love and spends his life helping others. He is the one who decides to lay out Sailor's body to teach Danis a lesson and "make him understand, if he can still understand" (p. 262). The role that he plays in the teaching of death explains the macabre name that he has chosen for himself: Toussaint, which means "All Hallows' Day" in French.

THE TWIN

Danis is almost never called by his name. He is more than just another character; he is the object of Antonio and Sailor's quest. He is disobedient and rebellious, murdering Maudru's nephew, abducting Gina and hunted by all the herdsmen of the region. When Sailor finds out what he has done, he describes him as a "mad lion" (p. 131).

For his enemies, his red hair is a sign that he is like the devil.

Danis says little for a long time. He has to face up to his father's death to become a man. When Antonio observes him taking his revenge, it suddenly hits him that the boy has grown up. The twin then has to take on the role of the "last man of the family" (p. 68). On the raft home, he plans to build the house that he promised his wife Gina, a little nervous because of his youth, but also eager to carry out his duty as a husband.

THE MAUDRU CLAN

Well before his first physical appearance, there are many signs which indicate that Maudru is an enemy and potential source of danger: he is the man who rules arbitrarily over the Rebeillard country, which the freedom-loving Antonio and Sailor do not like one bit. When they arrive on Maudru's lands, they learn that "Maudru doesn't want fires to be lighted on his pasture" (p. 41). However, when Antonio finally meets Maudru, he does not see the tyrant he was expecting but rather a bitter man with whom he can empathise.

The other leader of the clan, Gina, Maudru's sister, leads her men with an iron fist. Toussaint describes her as a manipulative, aggressive woman: "Not that she's quite indifferent about Mederic's death [...] but what she wants above all is fighting" (p. 219).

Not counting the herdsmen, there are another 30 or so people involved with the clan, according to Toussaint, notably the Demarignotte family and Delphine Melitta.

GINA

Maudru's daughter, Gina is engaged to Mederic, the son of old Gina, but she chooses to run away with Danis. The young girl appears to be determined and inflexible, the kind of woman who guides her husband towards logic and duty. From her very first meeting with Antonio and Sailor, her father-in-law, she hurls a wave of criticism at Danis, who she describes as a "girl-stealer" (p. 139) who has made her prisoner.

Gina is at the origin of the troubles in the Rebeillard country: she is the reason that Danis and Mederic fight. She criticises her husband for his instincts and his brutality, and his purely carnal attraction to her: "Your eye has never really been keen enough to get into me beyond my skin" (p. 175). She slowly reveals her ideal of love: a couple who care more about feelings and emotions than physical desire.

CLARA

When she first appears, this blind woman with eyes "like two mint leaves" (p. 53) is in the middle of "being delivered of a child in the brushwood, just like a sow" (p. 167). Of all the characters, she is the most savage and animalistic. As she lives in permanent darkness, her instincts are far more honed than those of Antonio, even though he is able to communicate with nature. She explains to Gina that "all the things in the world come to me in various places in my body" (p. 295).

There is something mysterious about Clara, symbolised by both her dead, elusive eyes and by the child that she had alone in the forest. While she seems ready to talk to Antonio at the end of the book, she eventually chooses to stay quiet. Just like nature, Clara is both fragile and strong, pure and murky. As a result, he falls head over heels for her: "She was all around him. Her blood touched his blood, her flesh against his flesh, mouth to mouth, like two bottles of wine that you empty one into the other and then turn upside down again, and they both glow with the same wine" (p. 309).

ANALYSIS

NATURE PERSONIFIED

In an article in the newspaper *L'Intransigeant* in 1932, two years before *The Song of the World* came out, Giono announced his plan to write a novel in which men would not take centre stage: "A river is a character. Running water [...], forests [...], fields [...]: all that is something more than a show for our eyes. It is a society of living things."[1]

Giono accomplished this with the help of two techniques in particular:

- On the one hand, he personifies nature with recurring metaphors which lend human characteristics to natural elements. For example, the river where Antonio bathes has muscles and the sun and the rain are described as walking through the country. These metaphors are complemented by a great number of comparisons, like the one on the first page: "It was

---

1. This quotation has been translated by BrightSummaries.com.

an aged oak, more sinewy than a man of the mountains" (p. 3).

- On the other hand, Giono also seems to associate each of his characters with either a natural element (water for Antonio, earth for Sailor), or an animal (Clara is compared to a sow). Instinct plays a large part in the many scenes which take place in the darkness, particularly Antonio and Sailor's walks. In a similar vein, Clara's explanations about her perception of things are an ode to the sense of smell.

CIVILISATION CONDEMNED

Antonio's happy little isle of jays is contrasted with a threatening town where a small group of people (the Maudru clan) make the law and subjugate the other inhabitants. There are several elements in the novel which emphasise this opposition between free, living nature and a dying, shackled society:

- In the Rebeillard country, habits are changing for the worse: men hunt men (the herdsmen who are looking for the twin) and not beasts (like Antonio and Sailor do).

- On the road to Villevieille, the two heroes come across a number of injured people, many of whom carry death with them (Clarissa, Maudru's nephew, Toussaint's patients).
- In the third part of the novel, while the characters are heading back south, the vocabulary shifts to focus on life. This can be seen particularly in the descriptions of nature: "Fish leapt in the river. A fox called out with a small plaintive yelp. Grey turtle-doves flew against the sun and the tips of their wings lit up" (p. 299).

A TALE OF A QUEST

In several ways, Antonio and Sailor's journey takes the form of a quest, beginning with the departure from their native lands and ending with their journey home. The object of this quest is the twin and, although Sailor is his father, it is Antonio who tends to take the lead and make rational decisions.

As in all quests, Sailor and Antonio are faced with a number of obstacles, which range from the hostility of nature to threatening herdsmen. Winter traps them in the Rebeillard country once they have found the object of their quest. This corresponds to a common feature of coming-of-age stories, when the hero is held back by an obstacle before they can make their way home.

Antonio and Sailor's journey also includes unexpected gains and losses. Antonio would never have imagined that he would meet his sweetheart alone in a forest. On the other hand, Sailor's death becomes the most dramatic shock of the quest, even though Junie's parting words seemed more like an omen than a farewell, as she pointed out that Antonio was taking away "the last man of the house" (p. 21).

Antonio and Sailor are inseparable for a good part of the journey. They overcome a series of obstacles which sometimes take them further away from their objective and sometimes bring them closer to it. The two are reminiscent of the duos often found in tales of quests, such as Don Quixote and Sancho Panza (unexpected mee-tings on the road, several stops, discussions in the forest), the heroes of Cervantes' (1547-1616) famous *Don Quixote*, even if the register is com-pletely different. The Greek poet Homer's (8th century BC) *Iliad* and *Odyssey* are also referenced a number of times throughout *The Song of The World*.

FROM ADVENTURE TO MYTH

Antonio is a character with an exceptional physique and character. In this respect, he is not unlike the mythical heroes of classic Greek literature, such as Odysseus from the *Odyssey*.

Giono is fascinated by Greek literature (his first novel, *Naissance de l'Odyssée*, or "The Birth of the Odyssey", is a rewriting of Odysseus' return to Penelope) and scatters relatively explicit references to it throughout the novel. The fire at the Maudru farm, for example, is reminiscent of the Siege of Troy. In a similar vein, the heroes' return home is rather similar to Odysseus' journeys.

The Song of the World also makes reference to other Greek myths:

- The Rebeillard country is full of oxen and Maudru is first described as "the ox-tamer", which recalls the god Mithras and the bull cult.
- In many respects, Antonio, the smooth-talking hero who is even able to communicate with plants, is very similar to Orpheus. Just as Orpheus was forced to combat the siren and Cerberus, Antonio also meets a fantastical

animal at the entrance to an unknown land, a "conger in fresh water" (p. 32) with "silent, gaping jaws" and "saw-like teeth" (p. 34). He is very loyal, and although he loses his Eurydice (Clara) on the way, he comes back to save her, whatever the cost: "Yonder, in front of that shadowy place. She does not know that I'll rush her into that" (p. 309), he thinks on the way home.

FURTHER REFLECTION

SOME QUESTIONS TO THINK ABOUT...

- Nature is a character in its own right in *The Song of the World*. Why can we say that it is also the main character?
- In what way does Antonio have the typical characteristics of a mythological hero?
- Study the female characters in *The Song of the World*. In what ways are they different and similar to each other?
- In *The Song of the World*, Giono seems to be condemning civilisation and exalting nature, which he believes is the only thing that can mend our broken society. Use your knowledge of philosophy to prove him right or make counterarguments.
- The French critic Pierre Citron wrote that "*The Song of the World* is a novel of mountains, not hills [...] It is also a novel about a river: the Durance [...] *The Song of the World* is a book filled with action and adventure. [...] Even

more so than Giono's previous works, it is a book about a rescue."[1] Based on your own understanding of the novel, develop this view.

- In *The Song of the World*, Antonio is loyal in friendship and in love. Analyse and compare these two themes in the novel.
- Toussaint tells Antonio that "There are truths you can sense [...] and there are truths which I know" (p. 173). Comment on this quotation.
- Compare the role and representation of nature (particularly in the South of France) in Giono's works and in those of another Provençal writer, Marcel Pagnol (1895-1974).
- Can Jean Giono be described as an environmental writer? Justify your answer based on your reading of *The Song of the World*.

---

1. This quotation has been translated by BrightSummaries.com.

We want to hear from you!
Leave a comment on your online library
and share your favourite books on social media!

FURTHER READING

REFERENCE EDITION

- Giono, J. (2000) *The Song of the World.*
  Trans. Fluchère, H. and Myers, G. California:
  Counterpoint.

ADAPTATION

- *Le Chant du monde.* (1965) [Film]. Charles Vanel.
  Dir. France: Les Films Marceau, Cocinor, Orphée
  Productions.

MORE FROM BRIGHTSUMMARIES. COM

- Reading guide – *The Horseman on the Roof* by Jean
  Giono.

- Reading guide – *The Man Who Planted Trees* by Jean
  Giono.

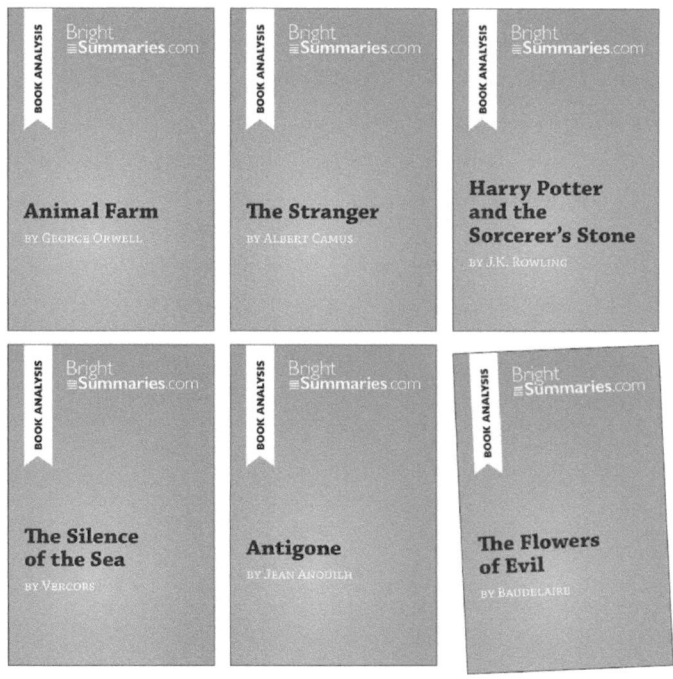

www.brightsummaries.com

Ebook EAN: 9782808000802

Paperback EAN: 9782808000819

Legal Deposit: D/2017/12603/468

Cover: © Primento

Digital conception by Primento, the digital partner of
publishers.